Scale While You Sleep

9 Automated Email Sequences That Can Grow Your Ecommerce Business 30% In 30 Days

Chris Orzechowski

Scale While You Sleep

Independently Published

Copyright © 2020, Chris Orzechowski

Published in the United States of America

200511-01605.2

ISBN: 9798679953956

No parts of this publication may be reproduced without correct attribution to the author of this book.
For more information on 90-Minute Books including finding out how you can publish your own book, visit 90minutebooks.com or call (863) 318-0464

Here's What's Inside...

Introduction 1

Chapter One:
The Right (And Wrong) Way
To Do Email Marketing 6

Chapter Two:
Where Do I Start? 20

Chapter Three:
Before the Sale Automations 27

Chapter Four:
During Fulfillment Automations 46

Chapter Five:
After Delivery Automations 61

Chapter Six:
Scale While You Sleep Success
Stories 76

Chapter Seven:
Here's How We Can Help Grow
Your Brand 85

Here's How You Can Scale Your
Ecommerce Brand While You Sleep 91

Introduction

A few years ago, I had a client who was barely using his email list. He was spending all his time worrying about his Facebook and Instagram ads.

He was doing a great job of making sales and growing his list with his ads but he wasn't doing anything with his customers after they purchased.

They sat there on his list, collecting dust while he ignored them and put all his focus into finding complete strangers he could sell to.

He spent so much money acquiring these customers (people who demonstrated that they liked his company's products) but he wasn't spending any time furthering the relationship with email.

That's like spending money to throw a big party and then refusing to talk to your guests once they arrive.

Crazy!

When I saw what my client was doing, I came in and set up a few basic automated email flows for him. After a short while, these automated email flows started generating around 25% of his store's revenue for the entire year.

He was kicking himself, thinking about all the money he left on the table over the past few years by NOT having these simple, automated email sequences in place!

Now, he was generating hundreds of thousands of dollars of extra revenue without working for it at all. We literally set up his sequences, made them live and then watched sales roll in.

Day after day, hour after hour, sales came in like clockwork, even while he was sleeping. This was a few years ago.

Those sequences we created back then are STILL pumping out sales for him, even to this day. And they'll run for years and years without him ever having to touch them.

Listen, one of the hardest parts of growing an Ecommerce brand is scaling to the point where you have enough cash flow and profit margin. Many brands watch their profits evaporate as they're forced to pay sky-high acquisition costs that come with paid advertising.

Some of the people running these brands think the only answer to their problem is to pump even more money into their ads. This problem is not unique. It's far too common, even with businesses that have been operating for years.

After working behind the scenes with dozens of Ecommerce brands, I noticed that most of them have their focus in the wrong place. They focus on their ads when they SHOULD be focusing on their email marketing.

I wrote this book so I could show YOU a few simple methods you could use to increase your sales while growing your profit margins and cash flow.

I created a simple system, which not only helps your brand make more money and increase profits but also provides an amazing experience for your customers.

When you follow the system I lay out for you in this book, you'll turn one-time buyers into loyal fans of your brand who want to buy from you over and over again.

I won't let you make the same mistakes that I've seen so many other Ecommerce business owners make.

At the end of the day, my hope is for you to experience the same kind of results my clients routinely experience from the work we do together at Orzy Media (www.OrzyMedia.com), my boutique Ecommerce email marketing agency.

I hope this book helps you explode your profit margins, make MORE sales while spending less on ads and ultimately have more cash flow in your business, more money in your pocket, and a lot less stress in your life.

Here's to Scaling While You Sleep,

Chris Orzechowski

Chapter One: The Right (And Wrong) Way To Do Email Marketing

Over the years, I've looked under the hood of a lot of different Ecommerce brands. What I've found might make your stomach churn.

More often than not, I find companies with HUGE lists (with tens of thousands of subscribers) who are lucky if they make a couple hundred bucks in sales when they send an email.

They're constantly running flash sales and offering huge discounts. They churn and burn through their customers, destroying relationships, and ruining any goodwill they had with their customers.

They POUND their customers with sale after sale until eventually people start to tune out and unsubscribe.

I've also seen situations where people aren't emailing at all or emailing once a month because that's what some "gurus" say is a best practice. These brand operators barely make any money because they're not staying in contact frequently enough.

If you fall into one of those camps, you're really doing a lot of harm for your list. Lucky for you, there's a better way.

Every Email You Send "Trains" Your Buyers To Behave A Certain Way

If you copy what most of the "big brands" are doing with their emails, you're shooting yourself in the foot. Allow me to shift your perspective on this. You might think to yourself: "Well, these companies have very nicely designed emails with HTML and all these pretty images and big buttons. Maybe we should make our brand's emails pretty, too!"

If you study what the big brands do, there's not really much copy in these emails. They tend to use heavy discounts and they're constantly running flash sales over and over again.

Two companies who come to mind who I've personally seen do this a lot are J. Crew and Brooks Brothers. I've been on their lists and have seen them use this exact strategy. Interestingly enough: they both filed for bankruptcy this year.

I guess all those aggressive and discount driven emails catch up to you after a while. This strategy just isn't going to work for you.

Clearly, it ruins big brands (many of which succeed in SPITE of their email strategy, until they sacrifice so much margin they file for Chapter 11). This strategy ruins small brands as well.

Obviously, there are many factors here. But I have to think that email marketing is definitely a big one, because you can't afford to continue to race to the bottom.

You can't afford to continually have your products on sale. People are smart. They understand what we're doing as marketers. If you train your customers to only buy when there's a discount, you can't be surprised when you can no longer sell without a discount. You have to change your strategy if you want to thrive and succeed.

Enough is Enough

People are inundated with crappy emails. They are just straight-up tired of seeing ads in their inbox.

A lot of statistics say that 50 years ago, people only saw a few hundred ads a day. Now we're bombarded with 5,000 or 10,000 ads every single day.

The inbox is an intimate sacred place. When you go into your inbox, you don't want to see a bunch of ads. You want to see an email from a friend or a colleague or a family member. Those are the emails that are going to get the most attention. They're going to get read and they're going to get a response.

There's a reason for that. If you're like most people, when you open an email and see a pretty header with a logo, a few header navigation buttons and a big hero image, you can smell the sales pitch coming from a mile away.

Before you even scroll down, before you even read what the email is about, your subconscious is warning you, *"This is an ad. This isn't important for me to see."*

Obviously, we are trying to sell with all of our emails. We're trying to help people with our products, our solutions, and the things we're selling.

There's nothing wrong with that. But we can do it in a way that builds some goodwill and trust that builds a relationship with your audience.

That way, people actually look forward to reading the emails you send, instead of having them think to themselves, *"This company is sending me another ad and they couldn't care less about me."*

The World's Most Powerful 1-2 Punch Ecommerce Email Marketing Strategy

I've talked a lot so far about the WRONG way to do email but what's the RIGHT way to do it? Well, my system for helping Ecommerce businesses grow faster with email is quite simple and a two part approach.

Think of it like a 1-2 punch combo. You "Pay Yourself First" with regular email broadcasts to your list and you layer on smart, behaviorally-triggered email automations to scoop up lost sales. That's it. Simple, right?

Pay Yourself First

As a business owner, I believe in paying myself first.

Before I spend a dime on Facebook, or Instagram, or YouTube, or Google and that meter starts running, I'm up early in the morning writing an email to my list so I can make some sales.

At the time of this writing, we currently have one brand as a client, where we're making six figures a month just by Paying Ourselves First with an email to his list four times a week.

We'll probably move to daily emails soon. When we do, we'll make even MORE sales. We Pay Ourselves First - by generating sales through email marketing BEFORE we give the social media ad platforms a dime of our money.

If all you took from this book was this ONE strategy, you'd be raking it in. But, my Pay Yourself First system is not what we're going to be discussing in this book. If you'd like to learn more about it, make sure you subscribe to my print newsletter at www.makeitrainmonthly.com)

What we ARE going to be discussing in THIS book is the second of half your email marketing game plan. Specifically, we'll be covering the magic of email automation.

Smart, Behaviorally Triggered Automations That Sell While You Sleep

When you create email flows like I'm about to show you in this book, you're going to be able to 'scale while you sleep' VERY fast. In fact, if you work fast enough and get all these flows set up, you might even grow your sales by 30% in the next 30 days. To be honest, 30% might even be an understatement.

We work with some brands that literally make more than 50% of their revenue from email marketing. Of course that might not be the reality for EVERY single brand in the world. But, imagine that, a brand that's doing $1,000,000 a year could feasibly be doing $2,000,000 (or more) if they started paying more attention to their email marketing.

When you look at it like that, growing 30% in 30 days seems like a pretty low bar to jump over. Again, this is not a PROMISE or GUARANTEE; not at all. I have to give the general disclaimer that every brand is different and it takes a lot of work to be successful no matter what you're selling.

If you're the kind of person who thinks you can buy this book, stick it under your pillow, and wake up tomorrow expecting a Rolls Royce to magically appear in your driveway, you might wanna read a different book. The stuff in this book does take some work and some effort. But it's work you only have to do ONCE and then it'll help bring in sales for DECADES.

The Main Difference in MY Approach

Most Ecommerce emails look more like billboards than they do emails. I like to do to things differently and make emails actually look like emails. Every email you send should come from a person (preferably YOU). It should have a conversational tone. It should feel personal. It shouldn't feel corporate and stuff, or bland or boring.

Every email is an opportunity to delight your customers and give them an unforgettable experience with your brand. Your emails shouldn't look (or feel) like an ad. Remember this.

Key Takeaway

Most business owners need to realize that there is so much money in their email list just waiting to be taken. The EASIEST way to scoop up some of this money is by implementing a set of behaviorally-triggered email automations. This is what's going to allow you to scale while you sleep.

As people on your list execute certain behaviors (like leaving things in their carts or checking out certain products or hitting a certain spending threshold to become a VIP) you have an opportunity to follow up with email to increase your sales and ascend the relationship with those customers. Essentially, if you do what I say in this book, you'll scoop up a lot of free money that's lying on the table.

Allow me to beat a dead horse for a second here:

Every single day you're not using a good, solid, proven email marketing strategy, you're leaving money on the table.

At my agency, Orzy Media (www.orzymedia.com), we set clients up with an email marketing systems that sell like crazy.

Suddenly, they're making an extra $500, $1,000 (sometimes more) every single day from email automations alone. It comes from these behaviorally triggered email sequences. You don't have to lift a finger once they're set up (unless you wanna start testing and tweaking).

Basically, it's an almost "set it and forget it" system. You set it up once, and the automations just run. Every single day that you do not have any sequences set in place, you're basically robbing yourself. Because you're losing money you could have easily had or recovered.

While advertising is important, business owners need to understand that advertising isn't everything. Sure, advertising is very important in getting traffic to your site and to your products. Obviously, to grow a business, you always need to be able to acquire more customers.

However, I've talked to many business owners who are able to run hyper-profitable Ecommerce brands WITHOUT needing to pay for ads. I spoke with one of them recently, a guy who owns multiple seven-figure Ecommerce brands that he runs pretty much by himself with maybe a handful of employees.

Basically, he told me he never has to spend another dime on advertising for the rest of his life because he has a decent enough sized list and he knows how to sell to them and keep them coming back over and over again. He has that business running, making sales, and supporting him, his family, and his team because he knows email marketing. That's really powerful, especially because everyone just wants to focus on Facebook, Google, YouTube, or Instagram.

Obviously, these are very good channels for acquiring customers, but you deepen and further that relationship through email. **That's where each customer's lifetime value is built.** That's where there are opportunities to recoup even more of your investment from your ad spend. If you have to pay to make a sale every time you want to make a sale, these acquisition costs will destroy your margins.

An email has no acquisition cost because you've already paid for that customer. You might have paid to acquire these customers two or three years ago - and you can still market to them all the time without having to pay another acquisition cost.

They're YOUR customers.

You bought the right to communicate with them, and they've stuck around because they like you and your brand.

Email marketing will probably be the one activity with the highest effective hourly rate for the time you invest in it. Now, remember, I'm not saying, "Don't focus on your front end; don't focus on advertising at all." What I am saying is the lion's share of your profits won't come from advertising. They'll come from dialing in your backend, with email.

Marketing Myth

One of the biggest myths in Ecommerce marketing is that you need to use a lot of branding with a lot of imagery, and have really pretty well-designed emails. We've tested this, time and time again, with many of our clients. Our customers seem to respond better when we're not burying the copy. We focus on the copy and the messaging by stripping down all those elements and getting people to focus on the words and the message we're trying to convey. Howard Gossage, a very famous Mad Men from the '50s and '60s had a great saying that explains WHY this works:

"People don't read ads. They read what interests them. Sometimes it's an ad."

If all you're ever doing is sending heavily branded, beautiful ads, you will turn off a lot of people. If you write interesting copy, so that people can connect with the content and stories and messaging, you're always going to get a much higher readership over time. You'll get much more retention and customer loyalty with your email marketing.

Chapter Two: Where Do I Start?

Let's Keep Things Simple

There's a lot of confusion in getting started with email because whenever you log into your email software, there are a LOT of buttons you can click. You've got your list, your segments, your broadcasts, your automations, and tags, your integrations, etc.

It can be a bit confusing. Luckily, we're going to simplify things for you. At my agency, we follow a checklist, making sure our clients follow a proven process to get them up to speed fast.

Let's assume you're starting at zero. You have a list and you're selling products on your site. As customers buy, they're being added to your email software. However, you're not doing anything at all in email marketing. The very first thing you want to do is start to set up some behaviorally-triggered automations, or 'flows' as they're called in Klaviyo, which is a popular Ecommerce email marketing software.

Starting with those basic flows is super important because every single day, people on your list are finding their way to your site and they're either doing or not doing things as they interact with your store. They're browsing and adding items to their cart. They're purchasing new items. Or, maybe they haven't purchased in a while and they're starting to churn.

These are behaviors we can capitalize on. Every single day, we can send relevant messaging to those people without YOU having to lift a finger. We can generate sales from those people, by following up when they execute certain behaviors.

The very first thing is to set up a few basic flows in your business. That way, you can start making more sales even while you're focusing on other things.

Can't I Just Google It?

Sadly, too many brand operators get their email marketing advice from random articles they find on Google. I've had clients tell me, "Well, I searched for email marketing best practices, and I saw these websites. I just tried to model what I saw the big brands doing."

I ask them, "Well, how did that work out?"

Their answer is always the same: "Not too well."

I can't say I'm surprised. Big brands are playing a different game with completely different rules. They are succeeding in spite of doing their marketing, not because of it. They might have five million people on their email list while you only have 20,000.

They also have three floors of people in the marketing department who can solve problems and craft new campaigns.

You need to focus on what's good for YOUR brand and stop worrying about what everyone else is doing.

You need to make sure what you're doing is leveraged and sustainable and, at least partially automated. That way, you can build an asset. You can build infrastructure in your business to keep you from being the one who has to wake up every single day and make the cash register ring. These flows are your assets that will bring in cash for you for the next 20+ years, completely automated. I can't stress how high the leverage is here.

Let's Play Monopoly

It really makes sense to focus on the basics, the things you can control. Things that will lead to you getting an ROI, not just for the money you spend on your email software but also for the time you invest. The cool thing is that all of these flows and the sequences I'll show you can be assets in your business.

These automations are like buying properties on the Monopoly board. Every single day, you're getting paid, whether you're there or not. The more automation you build, the more spaces you own on the Monopoly Board.

If one automation makes you $200 a day, that's pretty good. That means you're making about $6,000 a month. If you have ten automations and they're all performing about the same, now you are making $60,000 a month with the same amount of effort. You don't have to do anything to sustain that - just wake up and watch the sales roll in.

Key Takeaway

Every email you EVER send will be much more profitable if you have these automations in place. It's kind of like a pinball machine. Each customer you "launch" toward your website (from a broadcast email) can ping around from page to page, triggering sequences, increasing the amount they're going to spend with you. Once that starts happening, you have more cash flow to play with, which you can either take as profit OR invest back into the business.

Marketing Myth

Most people think they'll 'annoy' people if they send too many emails. The truth is, the only people who will get mad if you email too often are people who never wanted to buy from you in the first place.

Your best buyers will be the ones who love your emails and those are the only people who really matter.

I have had the pleasure of working with hundreds of businesses and speaking with their owners. I've NEVER once seen a list go to zero because someone has been emailing too often.

It's funny; I literally had a guy tell me once that if he started emailing every single day, he KNEW all 36,000 people on his email list would unsubscribe immediately.

I said, "I have never, in all my years, with all the people I've talked to; of all the businesses I've worked with; of all the times I've written daily emails for my clients, I have never seen or heard of this happening, ever."

We didn't end up working together - because I refuse to work with people who have such poor beliefs.

Chapter Three: Before the Sale Automations

Automating Sales

Before we get started, let me reassure you that setting up these sequences is not necessarily hard to do. Not everyone likes to do it, and that's totally fine.

Some people like to have a tech person go in and push all the buttons. Others like to have a skilled copywriter or email marketing expert actually write the emails.

I'm sure you understand the importance of copy, and where it can mean for your business. The better your copy, the more sales you make on the sequences.

Here's the cool thing though, if you currently have no sequences in place, just adding a basic sequence will be help capture more sales. Anything is better than nothing.

Remember, these automations are not going out to everyone on your list. They're *only* going to people who execute certain behaviors at certain times, which means, you're sending the right message to the right person at the right time with the right offer. Since you're not sending these automations to every single person (you're only sending them to people based on behavior) you tend to get pretty good results even if your copy is not exceptional.

If you're worried about getting started with this, don't worry. You could always get these automations in place and make them better later. The key thing is to get them moving as fast as possible because, as I said before, every single day you put this off is money you could have had.

We've literally worked with businesses that are now making an extra $1,000 every single day like clockwork, without them lifting a finger, from these automations. Just imagine that every single day; you're lighting $1,000 on fire that could have been in your pocket. That's the reality you're living in, every day you don't have these set up in your email software. So, just get some basic ones set up. If I had to pick only three for you to start with, it would definitely be what I like to call the "before the sale" automations.

Before The Sale Automation #1: Cart Abandonment Sequence

This first sequence is probably the lowest-hanging fruit in your business. Cart abandonment emails work incredibly well for Ecommerce, but I've actually done these with all kinds of companies - even companies who sell digital products. It doesn't matter what you sell - this sequence just WORKS!

There's so much money left in carts every single year; it's actually disgusting. It'll make your stomach turn when you hear the statistic I'm about to share. I can't remember the exact year, whether it's 2017 or 2018, but it is estimated that there were $4.6 trillion worth of goods left in online shopping carts that year.

Think about that number; it's an obscene, absurd amount of money being left in shopping carts. That is more than the economy of a number of small countries. If "goods left in abandoned carts" were a country, it would probably rate in the top 10 biggest economies in the world. That's how many transactions are not completed because carts are getting abandoned.

A lot of people are doing nothing about this problem in their own business. Or they have a very shoddy process for trying to recoup some of that money.

The cart abandonment sequence is basically just a sequence that triggers when someone goes to your website, and they're looking around your products. They find one or two they like, and they add the products to their shopping carts.

They start to check out, but for some reason, they don't complete the purchase. You've probably done this yourself. I know I've done it many times.

This is the thing to remember: people are doing this with your store, with your brand, with your website literally as you read the words on this page. People are getting to the one-yard line with your company and they're just not punching the order through. When your cart abandonment sequence fires, it gets people to go back to the shopping carts where the items are still waiting for them, so they can complete their order.

Industry statistics also say that 70% of shopping carts are abandoned. That's an average across all industries, products, and business sizes. We'll just use that number, although your industry might be a little bit higher or a little bit lower.

The fact is that the overwhelming majority of shopping carts are going to be abandoned, so you need to have a sequence in place that gets people back into it. If all you did was capture 10% of those sales, how much money would that add to your business?

This happens all the time, for many reasons you might not expect. Some business owners think, "If people are abandoning the cart, they just don't want my product." That's not true at all.

Life Happens

About six months ago, I was shopping for a gift for my wife. I was filling out my information, about to check out and complete my order. At the same time, I was also having renovation work done on my guest bathroom upstairs.

The crew at my house was jackhammering the tiles, and the walls started to shake. I figured everything was fine, so I kept shopping. But I completely forgot our wine glasses that were perched precariously behind me on the floating shelf. I didn't notice because I was sitting at the dining room table and working, thinking everything was fine.

All of a sudden - as I'm mid-checkout, buying this gift for my wife - one of the glasses fell and shattered into about a billion pieces. I spent the next 25 minutes, cleaning up all the glass. I had to stop what I was doing, get up, and locate the vacuum. This glass shattered right by our little mini-bar area, so I had to clean all the glasses. It was a process.

By the time I got back to my computer, I completely forgot about what I was doing. It's not like I didn't want the item I was shopping for. I still wanted it, but I got interrupted and then forgot about it.

Some variation of this story happens every single day, for so many different reasons. People's kids start screaming out of nowhere as they're shopping, or they get a phone call they have to take from work, or whatever. Maybe your customers just have questions, or they say, "I think this is what I want, but I need to do more research. I still want it, but let me make the decision tomorrow."

The fact is that people are very easy to capture if you just follow up. When we start sending these emails for clients, it's amazing how many sales get scooped up.

I have one client who sells a $6 product; this sequence generates anywhere from $500 to $1,000 a week, depending on the week and the amount of traffic going through, just from this one sequence alone. Again, the client is not doing anything to capture that money - he doesn't have to lift a finger. The sequence is set up. It runs in the background, and he just collects the sales.

It's great because it's money that would have just not been in his bank account because he wasn't following up with this sequence before. Now he is doing a great job of following up, and he's crushing it.

Mind you, that's with a relatively low-priced product. It doesn't necessarily change when it's a high-priced product. A cart abandonment sequence is just as effective, but if you have a higher-priced product or a mid-tier product, or at least a decent average order value, you could be capturing a higher amount of revenue depending on what you sell and the performance of your sequence.

If you could only get one sequence set up in your business, make it this one. Get it set up and you'll start seeing sales. Even if it's only one email long at first, that's fine. Ideally, we like to follow up with three emails. Depending on the number of SKUs you have, you can follow up a number of times, though.

I was on this one wine company's email list, Bright Cellars. They basically have one product: a wine membership. That's the only thing this company tries to sell.

After I signed up for their list but didn't complete my order, they literally sent me an email every single day for six months… until I finally bought. They did not stop following up. If you have a thousand different products, you're probably not going to do that. If you have ONE main product, you could do that. If you only have a handful of products, you can follow up over and over and over again until people finally buy or they leave, because there are only so many actions they can take. Even with just a three-email sequence, you'd be amazed by how powerful that can be.

A lot of people think, "If we send the first cart abandonment email and they didn't buy, they don't want it." That's not the case at all. By sending that second email the next day and the third email the day after that, you can capture 50% more sales just by having those two follow-ups. It's very powerful. Do it as a sequence. That is the lowest-hanging fruit in your business, the one thing you can implement today and absolutely start making more sales fast.

Before The Sale Automation #2: Browse Abandonment Sequence

The browse abandonment is an awesome sequence. We've been doing these for our clients, and they've just been absolutely crushing. It's pretty amazing to see the statistics. For some of these clients offering lower-priced products, they'll be making $1 - $1.50, sometimes even as high as $1.88/recipient.

Keep in mind, we've been seeing these numbers with some of our clients who sell very low AOV products. When you look at the numbers, you think, "Wow, if I just increase my traffic, increase my list..." Yeah. You'll be making a lot of sales. Obviously, that will differ depending on what you sell, and the quality of your products, the quality of your traffic, etc. There are always caveats, so it's not a guarantee or a claim or anything like that. These numbers just show some results we've been getting for our clients.

Obviously, a lot of factors go into that, but it's still super powerful because the browse abandonment sequence just follows up with someone if they simply "look" at an item but don't add it to their cart.

This happened to me the other day. As I was looking around for a shirt on a website, I thought, "This is pretty cool," and then I had to close the browser window because I had a phone call coming up in a few minutes and I needed to mentally prepare.

Again, it's not that I didn't want to buy the shirt. I just had something to do, so I couldn't go through the checkout process because I had to get ready for a phone call. That company sent me a series of browse abandonment emails... and I ended up buying the shirt because they reminded me to go back.

Sometimes people just need a little bit of a gentle reminder. Again, this is another three-email sequence that's nice and simple. We just follow up with these people. Keep in mind, you're not going to get 100% of people to buy. But the goal was not to get 100% of people to buy from that sequence.

The goal is just to increase the amount of income or revenue you're making through email without you having to do anything. Even if you're only getting 2% to 4% of people to purchase through that sequence, out of 100 people, if two people buy an average order value of $80 (which can happen every single day), it's $160 a day.

These small numbers add up. Combine that with cart abandonment, and now you're starting to see that the numbers can get pretty crazy.

That's a decent size average order value. But 100 people a day is not a huge amount of views for any decent-sized Ecommerce business. There are businesses out there getting 10,000 visitors a day to their sites. Some get 100,000 visitors a day, so the numbers can get really, really big. You could be scooping a decent percentage of these previously lost sales if you had these automations in place.

If you don't then you're essentially lighting $100 bills on fire instead of sticking them into your pockets, where they belong.

The browse abandonment recovers sales by providing a gentle nudge. We just show the product in the email, pulling it in dynamically for each person. We basically say, "Hey, did you have any questions? Were you interested in this?" Enough people say to themselves, "Yes, actually, I was. Thanks for reminding me," and then they buy it.

Sometimes we also use this as an opportunity to introduce related products. When someone viewed a product but didn't have time to look at another option that might be similar, we'll include some links in the bottom of these emails to those products as well. Those tend to get some clicks and make some sales.

It's just a nice, neat little sequence that runs in the background. You set it and forget it. It just churns out sales in a cool way, because you're not ramming it down their throats. We don't even use discounts. (I always try to sell without a discount, first.)

For most of the sequences, like the browse abandonment or cart abandonment, we don't use a discount. Just by reminding people about it, we capture a lot of sales we would have regularly lost.

Before The Sale Automation #3: Welcome Sequence

The welcome sequence gets sent out to people when they sign up for your list. It sells people who opt-in to your email list, organically, from your website. Obviously, a lot of Ecommerce brands will spend money to make a sale, and that's the primary way they people get onto their list as a customer instead of a prospect.

That's what you should be doing, but also, some organic traffic will always find your website. Maybe someone told one of their friends about your website, so they go in and type in the URL and check it out. You want a way for those people to get onto your list. You might have a pop-up or a floating opt-in bar. You might have an exit pop. All these things work well.

When people do get onto your list, you don't just want them to sit there while nothing happens. You want to put them through a sequence of emails that introduces you, tells them a little about your brand, and ideally, it'll share your origin story, too.

I usually like to include that in the very first email, because people always love hearing those origin stories. They help humanize your brand and build some resonance. For certain brands, when you know their story, and you can tell other people about it, you feel educated. You feel cool, like you're 'in the know.' And you feel a stronger bond than to these brands that don't have a cool story.

Another email you can include in that sequence is one where you demonstrate how your products are different than other options out there. You could also include social proof. You can dimensionalize your product's benefits and show ways they're being used.

You can use an emailing this sequence as an opportunity to introduce subscribers to your various categories of products, then, unpack the different categories and help people understand which products are right for them. It's probably too much to include in this book, but you could use a lot of different email frameworks, email types, and formulas in that welcome sequence.

(If you'd like to learn more about my favorite email formulas and frameworks to use in your welcome sequence, get my Pay Yourself First course by going to makeitrainmonthly.com).

The whole goal of the welcome sequence is to get people to make that first purchase.

I'm not saying this as a blanket recommendation. You'll have to make your own decisions based on your brand, but some brands will offer a 10% or 20% off coupon if you join their list and then they get put into their welcome sequence. The goal of that welcome sequence, obviously, is to make that first purchase. You want to get them to use that coupon code, but not everyone is ready to buy.

A decent number of people will be ready to buy, absolutely, because they signed up for a coupon code. A lot of them are obviously thinking, "I want to buy," so you want to get them to use it instead of letting that opportunity go to waste.

Here's the thing though, you also want to use this sequence as an opportunity to share your story stories, to build a bond, and to begin to form an image in their mind of who you are as a brand. That's what will keep them coming back for more. As I said, you don't have to use a discount. There are many different lead magnets or offers to get people onto your list.

I have a client who gets people onto his list because he raffles off a gift card to his store every single month. That means he doesn't have to give a discount to every single person, destroying his margins and training his buyers to only buy from discounts.

It doesn't happen too often with welcome sequences, but if you do that with EVERY email you send, it will definitely happen. It's totally fine to do that with just the welcome sequence, without having discounts in every single email people get from you in the future.

Anyway, because this brand I'm referencing here is more high-end and luxury-focused, this client of mine likes to just raffle off a gift card. His list has grown by tens of thousands of people over the years with just that one little offer. It works really well. It gets people in and gets them buying. It starts to tell the stories and build that bond with the subscriber right off the bat.

Key Takeaway

You want to get all of these sequences before that first sale is usually made. Obviously, the browse abandonment, the cart abandonment, will also go to people after they have purchased once. But these are the lowest-hanging pieces of fruit for your Ecommerce business. After you set these sequences up, they're just going to crank out sales for you around the clock without any effort on your part. You want to get those set up as soon as humanly possible.

Chapter Four: During Fulfillment Automations

During Fulfillment Automation #1: The Order Confirmation Email

The order confirmation sequence will definitely not be your highest-performing in terms of raw top-line revenue, but this might be one of the most important emails you ever send. Right now, your customers are getting order confirmation emails, but they probably suck.

They're usually super simple and sound something like this: "Hey, thanks for your order. Here's your tracking number, here's your receipt, and here's our support email, and have a good day." If that's it, you're doing the bare minimum. And you're wasting a HUGE opportunity to build your brand and make sales.

People don't think about those things, like optimizing this one 'seemingly unimportant' email automation. But here's why you SHOULD put some focus into this one. At my agency, we recently wrote an order confirmation email for a client, and he is just ecstatic.

Multiple times each week, I wake up with an email from this client of mine. He keeps forwarding us emails from his customers who just got the order confirmation email. The replies are always like, "Oh my God, this is the best email I've ever gotten from a company. I love you guys. You're so funny. You're awesome."

Our client is just gushing. He's even starting a positive feedback file for all of these comments because he just loves all the feedback he gets from these emails. The order confirmation email is just an email telling a story about how excited and happy you are that they just placed an order with your company.

Usually, you want to send this the first time someone buys. Obviously, if they've bought from you seven times and they get the same email seven times, it might get a little redundant. It might be overkill. This should ONLY go out the very first time someone buys.

On the next page is an example of what this email looks like, for one of our clients who sells an odor eliminating spray for people who smoke weed.

==================================

Subject line: Who's awesome? [FIRST NAME] is awesome!

Hey [FIRST NAME],

We were just about to get ready to take a little smoke break here in the office, when all of a sudden I checked my phone...

DING!

I swiped over to check the notification, and I couldn't believe what I saw...

"No way...", said Carl.

"It FINALLY happened...", Nate uttered in disbelief.

"It can't be...", replied the new guy (whose name I haven't learned yet).

But there it was, right on the screen... "[FIRST NAME] FROM [TOWN/CITY] JUST PLACED AN ORDER!"

Carl sat down and started rolling the fattest celebratory blunt you've ever seen. Nate pulled out his original edition *Doggystyle* vinyl record and blared it through the office. The new guy ran out to pick up a case of 40's so we could celebrate this monumental occasion. We all high fived each other because we're pumped up to finally have YOU as a customer.

Don't worry, once the celebrations die down, we'll pack your order and ship it straight out to you.

If you have any questions about your order, just hit reply.

It's great to welcome you into the [COMPANY NAME] family, [FIRST NAME].

[SIGNATURE]

P.S.

As another way of saying THANK YOU for becoming a [COMPANY NAME] customer… we'd like to give you a 10% off coupon to use on your next order of $40 or more:

Click here to get 10% off your next order (use the code XXXXXX at checkout)

================================

See how much fun this email is? My clients and customers LOVE this email. Once they order and read this email there's a much higher chance they'll keep coming back to buy again.

When you write one of these emails, they really make an impression. They're so over the top. There are characters and chaos that ensues because they saw your order come through, and everyone started cheering and clapping and popping champagne. When you have a fun, exciting, lighthearted, funny order confirmation email, you just build fans for life. I call it a 'Perfect First Impression email'.

I covered this in one of my *Make it Rain Monthly* newsletter issues (makeitrainmonthly.com). I wrote all about this and broke down my process for how to do it, including a number of examples of how you can create one for your own company.

Anyway, this email trains people. It says, "Hey, pay attention to our emails. Our brand is different from everyone else. We're fun and exciting. You're going to like the rest of the content you see." People get these order confirmation emails, and they go through what I call the '**Virtuous Cycle of Standout Emails**'.

Basically, people buy a product, they get an email, and they say, "Wow, this email made me laugh," or "This email is so clever. I've never seen anything like this before." They say to themselves, "I like this company." Then, they say, "I can't wait to buy from this company again." Then they buy and they get more good emails from you and the cycle repeats over and over. Around and around we go.

Each time they spend more and more money with you, and they're coming back for more. They're looking forward to more emails from your company because they're always looking to see what you say next.

Another side benefit of doing this: When you have this email in place, your customers are probably telling other people, "Oh my God, check out this email I got from this company." They're forwarding it to their friends, showing it to their coworkers at the desk next to them at work. It's very important. It's a huge brand-building piece.

We also put offers in these emails. We don't get a super high number of sales, but even if you're making an extra $20 to $50 to $100 bucks a day, this is money you weren't capturing before. You should always include an offer as a ride-along with that email.

A lot of times, these emails will get 50% to 90% opens because everyone looks for their order confirmation. I know I feel a sense of unease until I see the order confirmation going through, and I'm sure you're the same way.

I think to myself, "Did it charge my credit card? Did it charge twice? Did it charge at all? Did it work? Do I need to go back?" It's this panic moment for 30 seconds until that email hits your inbox.

That panic moment is met with this awesome order confirmation email that is over the top and makes people laugh, and they love it. It turns them into a fan for life because it hits them right in the emotions.

During Fulfillment Email #2: The Before It Ships Email

This is a cool email. Not everyone uses this one, but we've had great success with the clients who have implemented it. Either immediately or a few hours after someone buys, you can actually send them an upsell email.

This "Before It Ships" email basically says, "Hey, I just want to say thanks so much for your order. Just so you know, we're about to ship it out. Would you like us to throw in another unit of whatever you just bought?"

Sometimes, depending on your business, you could even ask them if they want to buy an ancillary or accessory product, something that makes the original product work better. You could just include an offer to buy anything else and maybe they get a discount on it before their order ships out.

We did this for one client, who was making anywhere from two to four sales a day from this one email automation alone.

Again, they were still growing when we implemented this, but those two to four sales a day wound up being about $100 to $200 extra daily revenue.

If you extrapolate that, even if it's only $100 a day in extra revenue, that's $36,500 a year at a minimum... on the low end. There were days when we made four or five of those sales from this one simple automated email. It gets people to increase the order value, increase the lifetime value, and you're actually helping them get more products into their hands that can help solve their problems.

It's not like you're ruthlessly reaching into their pocket. If you have a good product that will help them solve a problem and if getting another unit would help them even more, it's your DUTY to make that sale. You just make the offer and see what happens. You could upsell them into another product. You can upsell a bigger, better version of the product, or you can cross-sell an accessory product or a product that works well with what they just bought. You have a lot of options here. And it works really well.

During Fulfillment Automation #3: Post-Purchase Review Gathering Email

Why is this such an important sequence to have? Well, a lot of times, we look at reviews before we buy a product. I know I do this. My wife does this. Pretty much everyone I know does this. We always think, "Well, what are other people saying?"

Obviously, the company is going to say nice things about their own products. Why wouldn't they? They're not going to trash their own products. So what do other neutral third parties have to say, people who have actually bought the stuff before, and who don't work at the company? Gathering reviews provides incredible social proof.

I think I read a statistic that 80% or 90% of people will read reviews before they make a buying decision about something online. It's super important. Also, how many times have you just asked your friends or colleagues, your coworkers, or family members, "Has anyone tried ____ out?"

People always ask people they trust. They want to get someone else's opinion. As the business owner or the marketer, you need to find a way to incentivize people to include those reviews.

Just remember that most people are not writers. And most people are busy. You can't just say, "Hey, leave us a review," and then that's it. We can't expect people to just find their way to your product review page on their own.

Here's what you do…

Try sending out an automated email after a certain amount of time passes, once they've had a chance to not only receive the product but also to use it.

If it's a pair of shoes, they'll probably want to wear them once or twice. If it's another kind of product, they might need some time to use it and try it out. Then, in this email you send them, you want to ask them what they think about it. You can incentivize these people to get them to respond. This is one of those times it definitely does make sense to offer someone an incentive, like a discount or a credit, if they leave a review.

Obviously, they're going out of their way to help you out, so you should go out of your way to help them out. An easy way to do this is to say, "Hey, leave us a review. We'll give you X percent off (or an X dollar credit) towards your next purchase." You'll get a number of people to not only leave reviews and give feedback but they'll also wind up making a second or third purchase because of it.

A lot of Ecommerce businesses suffer from this retention problem. They can make the sale the first time, but making the second or the third sale, getting over that hump from one-time to two-time buyers (or getting people to become multi-buyers) is very hard for them.

Offering incentives is a great way to increase sales while also generating feedback and reviews. We're going to assume you are selling something good and valuable that works, that's useful, that people love.

We're assuming you have a good product, and people had a good experience. If that's not true, then none of this matters anyway. If you're not selling a good product, you won't be in business for a long time.

If your products are awesome, you're going to get a lot of great feedback. Sometimes you might even get negative feedback. That's not a bad thing because if there is something wrong with the product, or with the way it ships, you would want to know. You want that feedback.

Kevin Rogers, my mentor and copywriting coach (copychief.com) always says:

"The most valuable thing you could ever have with your audience is a dialogue."

I think that's super important. By getting those reviews and that feedback, by hearing what people have to say, that will help you improve as a business owner. It will improve your products and your offers and make them absolutely irresistible. It will help you sell even more in the long run.

Key Takeaway

These post-purchase automations are super important. They happen right after the sale. They definitely help you make sales, but they also go a long way toward building the bond you have with your customers and keeping them around.

Retention is so important. All these emails are designed to help your customers keep coming back to buy again by building a bond. They make good money, and they build a ton of goodwill.

Chapter Five: After Delivery Automations

After Delivery Automation #1: The VIP Sequence

Everyone talks about the 80/20 rule: 20% of your customers are probably buying 80% of your products. I think that holds true for just about everything. It's very hard to do business nowadays without hearing about the 80/20 law or the 80/20 rule. Within your own customer list, 20% of your customers probably account for 80% of your revenue. I can drill down even further.

Your VIP customers (the top 10%) are probably accounting for about 50% of your revenue. If you've read any books on the 80/20 rule, you know that the math holds true. The top 10% of your list is your most valuable customers. These are people who spend the most money, the people who come back and buy over and over again.

We like to make those customers feel special. We like to encourage and reward their good behavior, and thank them. Good behavior, in this case, means: buying more and more. We recently wrote a VIP email campaign for one of our clients. It was a 'longer copy' email. We basically told them because of their recent purchase they became one of our absolute favorite customers.

We said we're building a statue in their honor, and we had a big party in celebration. It was a fun, kind of silly email... not unlike the order confirmation email featured earlier in this book. It's a little cute and goofy, but it makes the reader feel special. If a customer buys a few times, they'll probably like being acknowledged, even if it's done privately in an email.

Case in point:

Many years ago, when I was a bartender at a local shot and beer joint, there were regulars who came in all the time. There was one guy who had made a ton of money, and he just threw it around like it didn't matter. He would give us $100 tips sometimes just because he just didn't give a crap. He didn't have a wife or kids… so he'd just blow money at the bar without a care in the world. (I'm sure it also helped that he was really into the female bartenders I worked alongside.)

The thing is, even though this guy would spend money like it was nobody's business, we STILL comp'd him drinks from time to time as a way to thank him. After all, the guy was a whale. There were nights when his tab would be 10% of ALL our sales for the entire night. One guy!

We obviously wanted to keep him around so he'd continue to spend with us. As a bartender, I learned that a lot of those regulars just want to be recognized.

They were there every day. The regulars always had the biggest tabs. They didn't care about the money they saved from you comping them a drink, as much as they cared about being recognized. It gave them status among the tribe.

I think this holds true for Ecommerce. When you buy from a company three or five or six times, and then you get an email that recognizes you as a VIP customer, you feel special.

We can go one step further in these emails and say, "We'd actually like to get your opinion on how to make our brand even better." And then we send them to a quick survey. These VIP customers think, "Whoa, I'm not just a special customer; they're asking me for help now, too." If that doesn't build a bond with the company, if that doesn't make you feel like you are part of the family... then I don't know what will.

We actually set up a survey, and in this VIP email, we said, "We'd love for you to fill out this survey and tell us how we can serve you even better. And, by the way, we're also going to give you 25% off for being so awesome. And you can use this code whether you fill out the survey or not." You can make your own determination about whether you want to give a gift, a credit, a bonus item, a discount, etc. Whatever it is, we like to give them some kind of reward for being a VIP.

Basically, the criterion is if someone has spent over a certain amount of money and/or bought a certain number of times from you. We want to reward those customers, so they do more of that. Out of all the people on your list, your VIPs are probably the people who will MOST LIKELY buy and spend more.

Again, this won't be the person who hasn't opened any of your emails in the past 90 days. The VIP will be the person who's bought from you seven times in the past year so we reward them for that so those behaviors continue.

These sequences are always pretty profitable. They build a lot of goodwill and strike a bond with your customers because they like being recognized and rewarded. It makes them just go crazy.

These are the people who will spread the word about your brand. They're sneezers. Even just from doing one small action like that, the sequence has so many ripple effects. They're going to share your stuff and ultimately buy more.

After Delivery Automation #2: Cross-Sell & Up-Sell Automations

After someone has bought, there's always a time when they might be ripe to buy again, and there are lots of ways to encourage this next purchase to happen. Maybe you sell a consumable. Someone's almost run out of their olive oil or face cream or bone broth (or whatever it is).

They've eaten 27 loaves of bread in the past month, and now their olive oil bottle is empty. They need to buy more. Say it's a 30-day supply. Maybe on day 20 or 21 after they've received it, once they're almost done with it, we'll send them an email to get them to re-up and buy some more. This is another way you can do this too, if you don't have a consumable.

Klaviyo has this cool feature, which will work differently for each business. It's not a perfect science, obviously. But based on the data from your customers and each customer's profile on your system, it can kind of predict when they might be ready to make their next purchase.

You can send an email, triggered by your customers' predicted date of next purchase, that upsells them to get more of the product or to cross-sell other products. "Hey, you tried the skin cream. Why not try the body lotion?"

If that's what you're selling, you could sell more of the same, or sell a bigger package of the same. You could sell people into a continuity program. You have a lot of different options, but they're basically about getting people to commit to that next purchase. Definitely a good one to test out.

After Delivery Automation #3: Win-Back Sequence

The win-back sequence is an email sequence sent to people who have not bought from your store in a long time. They haven't bought from you for 30 to 60 to 90 days. It could even be longer, depending on the sales cycle or how long the supply of your product lasts.

Maybe these customers just haven't made a purchase in a while, and you want to pull out all the stops to get them to buy again. If you can get them to come back and make another purchase, you might be able to reset their life cycle and get them to start buying from you regularly.

Certain companies will experience varying success with this sequence depending on their customer lists or their products. This probably won't be your most profitable sequence, just because these people have demonstrated they might not want your product as much as you'd like.

This is one of the sequences that get triggered by a customer NOT executing a certain behavior (buying). They haven't bought in a while, so we want to give them an incentive to come back and place an order. This is definitely a place where you'd like to use a discount, because if this segment of customers haven't bought from all your other marketing emails... you need to do something to shake the box a little bit to try to get people off the fence.

You could run some kind of deadline-driven promotion over a period of 24 hours. You can make the discount a little bit bigger each time you do it. Basically, you pick a frequency. Send one email at 30 days, offer a discount, and try to get them to buy.

If they don't buy, send another email at 60 days, offer a slightly bigger discount, and try to get them to buy. If they don't buy from that one, send them one at 90 days, and offer the biggest discount yet. Then you determine what you want to do with those people. You can choose to move them to an unengaged list or continue to market to them.

Again, it depends on what you're selling and how often. If you're selling a mattress, people don't buy them that often. If they haven't bought in 90 days, it's not necessarily a problem. It really depends. If you sell a consumable, and after 90 days they still haven't made another purchase, that person might be churned.

I'm a big fan of Dean Jackson. I love all his philosophies and methodologies when it comes to email. He's very famous for citing this study indicating the timing of when people are going to buy:

'Every customer will buy either now or not now. About 85% of people are going to buy not now. They're going to buy later. Most leads that raise their hand and express interest in a product are going to buy between 90 days and two years.'

I definitely think that's true. At least it's been true with my own email list.

A good buddy of mine, Ross O'Lochlainn, (author of *Open Every Day*, a fantastic book; conversionengineering.co/open-every-day-book) had me do a little experiment with my own list one time. He had me calculate the "time to purchase" of my customers. I compared the date when a customer initially subscribed to my list to the date when they finally bought my course and it was 4.53 months. Pretty crazy, right?

I had some people who bought 14 months after joining my list. They read my emails for 14 months before finally deciding to buy. All this is to say that we can't always assume people are NEVER going to buy again if they don't buy for a while.

But we want to follow up with this win-back sequence to scoop up as much low-hanging fruit as possible. So, with this sequence after 120 days or 180 days go by, if they haven't made a purchasing decision from your Ecommerce brand and all the emails you sent to make the sale, which might just mean you have to really shake the box to win them back.

Again, it's not going to happen to every single person that goes through it, but you will capture a percentage. You will recoup some revenue that could have been going into other peoples' cash registers.

Key Takeaway

These are sequences where you can really extend the lifetime value of your customers much, much further. Again, if you are spending money on advertising (like a lot of Ecommerce brands) every extra sale you can get out of a customer just lowers the average cost of the acquisition or your expense to attract that customer.

If you have to spend $50 to get someone to buy a $60 product, you're only making a $10 profit. If you can get three or four more sales out of them with all these backend sequences and automations, then maybe throughout the lifetime of that customer, you still spent the same $50 to acquire them, but now they've spent $240.

Obviously, you received a much better ROI on all your marketing spend.

Again, you could set and forget all these things, but you don't want to completely forget about them.

You'd like to optimize them, keep testing things, and pushing the conversion percentage as high as possible.

Usually, you don't have to spend a lot of time because these automations are just set up to run over and over and over again. Every day, they sell while you sleep.

That's what will help you scale while you sleep. You're going to be generating sales. You'll be waking up and seeing more cash going into your bank account. You're going to make a decision. You're going to say, "I can reinvest this cash flow into growth, and pump it into my front end advertising, to acquire even more customers."

When you get more customers, they'll go through your backend email system and be worth even more. They're going to make more sales. It's a flywheel. That's how you scale faster; by having this back end that makes every customer worth 10% to 30% to 50% more than if you had no email marketing.

A lot of people might read the title of this book and say, "30% in 30 days? That's a big number." For some clients who start doing email marketing after doing nothing… their business doubles practically overnight. It's really not that tall of an order.

If you're not doing anything at all, it's not unreasonable to expect that you can make some big gains really fast with just some basic emails. Again, if you're super dialed in with email already, you probably won't see as much explosive growth. But it all depends on the strategy, on the copy, on your ability to execute and get these things set up right.

You can find tons of money in your business every single day. It's not hard to find. All of these sequences can reach out and find this money for you. You just have to set these sequences up and start bringing in the cash.

Marketing Myth:

"Is discounting in my emails good or bad?"

The answer depends on the context, or on your overall strategy. I would recommend erring on the side of not offering discounts so that when you DO strategically offer them to certain subscribers based on behaviors they have executed with these behavioral sequences, they pack that much more of a punch.

If all you ever do is send discounts, people become blind to them. And eventually, they don't buy unless they see a discount. We call that living in "Discount Hell." If your business doesn't discount very often, the one or two times when a discount comes into your subscriber's inbox, they will act on it. It's going to be that much more powerful.

Chapter Six: Scale While You Sleep Success Stories

Everything I've shared with you in this book is applicable to all businesses across the board. No matter whether you're a startup, a solopreneur, or have a company of 500+ employees, the core concepts remain the same.

Let me tell you some customer success stories. One client I worked with long ago (a luxury brand) wasn't sending a lot of emails. My client's mentality was that he didn't really want to bother the subscribers, and he was very adamant about that.

I said, "Hey, that's totally fine. I understand. Obviously, I'd prefer if you sent more, but what if we just set you up with the suite of behaviorally-triggered automations so we'd only be sending emails to a small segment of your list each day?" For this client, we set up a set of automations designed to help him scale while he slept. These automations took a little bit of testing and optimizing, to get them to a level of conversions we were happy with.

But soon, about 25% of every dollar that came into his business was coming from one of these automated email sequences. Keep in mind that we're not talking about broadcasts. This was just from email automation. He didn't have to work for these sales... at all! Think about that. If you have a $1,000,000/year business and you're making 25% from your email automations, then that means you're making $250,000 from automations that were running while you slept or, while you were on the beach relaxing.

Basically, his suite of automations was a combination of the sequences we've outlined in this book. It's not just theory. This stuff absolutely works.

Less Discounts, More Profit

Another client I worked with had a very basic and lackluster email copy. Their automations were working okay, but they were really converting at a very low rate. It wasn't really reflecting the brand voice client wanted to convey.

Their sequences weren't really designed to make connections with the customers, subscribers, and leads. We came in and overhauled all the automations. We knew that some better copy could just blow it out of the water for this company.

We still used discounts occasionally because the client wanted to use them. But I had to really encourage them to stop offering discounts in EVERY email. They were a little nervous because they said, "We don't know if people will buy unless we offer them a discount."

We actually did split testing with the discount vs non-discount sequences. One sequence had an email that offered a 15% discount if you completed your order that day. That email was doing pretty well for them, actually. They were making a lot of money from it, but for every single person being converted through that email, they were basically taking a 15% hit on the margin sales.

We said, "We can get more people to convert with OUR sequence and generate more revenue from our sequence without using that discount." When we tested it out, we were making more money, top line, from our sequence.

Not only were we beating them in the split test, but we were also doing it without the discounts. Not only was our sequence earning them more money without the discount, but also we were able to get them more profits. Our sequence was 15% more profitable because ours didn't have to use a discount to close the sale. It just goes to show that if you have good copy, you have this opportunity in a strategy that can generate a lot of money for your brands on autopilot.

Good Gets Better

Another one of our clients was actually doing a great job. They weren't actually spending any money on paid advertising, but they had a very hungry list of awesome products that sold like crazy. Granted, once we took over their account we were able to double what they were doing before in terms of broadcast revenue, which was really, really cool.

Every time we sent an email, people were so happy with these products that they just couldn't get enough of them. We were crushing it through our broadcast strategy. We were just including more stories, making the copy a lot better, and doing some strategic things with their email templates. We were stripping them down a little bit, pulling in some dynamic products at the right times.

Even though we were doing well with the broadcasts, they had no automation, and nothing was set up when we first started. So we set up a browse abandonment sequence as soon as we started working together.

After the first 24 hours, they were making about $1.22 from the browse abandonment per recipient. It's only gone up from there. They were just absolutely crushing it because, as they did the broadcast, they were making sales from those emails.

If they sent 500 clicks from email, they might only get in about 20 to 30 sales, which is not a bad amount of sales. Then the browse abandonment captured another few dozen people through that sequence through the automation.

People were going and looking at the products. Even if they didn't buy directly from the broadcast, we followed up over the next few days with the browse abandonment. We set up other sequences that did well for them, too, but just that one sequence was cranking out sales for them every single day.

It's not really about what you make in a day.

It's about extrapolating, seeing if you can make an extra $100,000 or $200,000 (or more) each year from your automations. If you make an extra $1,000 a day, that's $365,000 a year.

If everything in your business stayed the same, but you made an extra $365,000 for which you didn't have to pay any acquisition costs, what would you do with that money? That would be life-changing money for most business owners.

We're not saying you have to go out and use these automations to make $100,000,000 next month. Obviously, that would be great. If you have a small business or growing Ecommerce business, it could give you the cash you need to make key hires or replace yourself for certain roles. It could give you the cash you've needed to take a vacation, to save for your kid's college fund, save for your retirement, or buy the dream house you want.

Again, I'm not making claims or promises. I'm just saying there's money that could be yours, and it's flying by every single day. If you just had some of these automations set up, it's like a salesperson who works for you around the clock, going out and recovering this revenue without you having to do a thing.

Post COVID-19

The worldwide pandemic was one of the greatest boons for Ecommerce, maybe ever. Obviously, it was a very terrible thing. It's horrible that people are dying; it's very unfortunate what happened to many small businesses.

But I need to be objective here and look at the data. Even though we were all on lockdown; everyone still had to buy things from somewhere. If you couldn't really leave your house, the only option you had was to buy online.

Some of my clients made more money during the pandemic than ever before in their business. It was absurd, but they had products to sell and a hungry audience.

People everywhere were on lockdown. They couldn't just go and buy from their local retail stores. They were essentially FORCED to buy online. Here's what's really crazy...

It takes three to six weeks or so to build a habit. At the time of this writing, the pandemic has lasted for four or five months now and it's still going on at the time of this writing. How many people will never go to the grocery store again, now that they've started ordering groceries online? How many people switched to buying from online brands because they couldn't shop at the regular store they liked?

Now they've found an online company they're comfortable with, a lot of people have decided to just keep buying from these online brands they've now found. For Ecommerce, that was the biggest boon ever. I don't think it's going to slow down anytime soon. I think the age of Ecommerce is just getting started. I think if you use the methods I lay out in this book, you are going to be finally able to scale while you sleep.

Chapter Seven: Here's How We Can Help Grow Your Brand

If you have an Ecommerce business with an email list and if you know you're not utilizing it as well as you should... and, if you want to make more sales while also building a great bond and a lot of goodwill with your subscribers and customers... then today is your lucky day.

At my agency, Orzy Media (www.orzymedia.com), we help Ecommerce brands predictable revenue and growth through email marketing.

If you're interested in working with us, you can fill out an application to work with us by going to www.orzymedia.com.

Please note: It's very expensive to work with us. We don't just work with anyone. We only take on a handful of clients each year so that we can go really deep with our brands and do excellent work.

Once you apply, if we think you're a good fit, we'll tell you what it's like to work with us and how we can help you grow your brand. You can sit back while our team of experts go in and do our thing.

We do the tech and write the copy. We set up all the email templates and do the segmenting. We'll make sure it works right, it runs right, and make sure your emails go to the right people at the right time. We'll recover tons of revenue for you without you really lifting a finger. How much is it to work with us? A lot, but what you're going to pay us is a fraction of what we think we can generate for you.

So, if you want to hit the big easy button, you can just hire us, and we'll do everything for you.

Go to www.orzymedia.com and apply today.

What Are You Waiting For?

It's my hope that you open your eyes to what is possible with your business. I know how hard it is to start a business, to bootstrap it and grow it, to get it to a level where it's doing well enough to support you. Along the way, there are roadblocks and obstacles and fires to put out; it's tough. It's definitely not easy.

My whole goal with this book was to show you that things can be a little bit easier. You can have a little bit less stress and a little bit more cash flow. You can have some more cushion and security. You can stabilize your revenue so that you're not dependent on ad platforms that don't have your best interests at heart. Email lists are the ONLY true marketing asset you own.

No one can ever take your list from you. Your ad account can get shut down before you stop reading this book. You can log on to Facebook and see that your ad account was shut down for no reason; it might take two weeks before it's back up, and that's completely out of your control. The only reason I'm saying that is because I know people who have experienced this issue. They had perfectly good products but were shut down for no reason.

When you're using someone else's platform, you are beholden to them and whatever they want to do. You have NO control. Other people I know have been running ads successfully, and everything is going great. Then suddenly, their CPAs skyrocket for no reason as they're trying to scale up their ad spends. It's frustrating to watch. But it DOES happen, all the time.

If you implement these email marketing sequences, you'll build a moat around your business. You won't be beholden to any ad platform.

You know you have security and stability in your business; you will be able to generate cash flow and sales and revenue and profits, literally on command. Most importantly, there will be more profit in your business every single day without fail, whether you are working or not working.

Whether you're on vacation or whether you are home in the office, it does not matter. That is the power of email marketing automation and what it can do for your Ecommerce business. The only thing you need to do is get it set up.

Once that's set up, you are building a moat around your business so no one can take you down. You will become impervious to all these things experienced by your competitors because they won't be doing email marketing at the level and quality that you are. Even if you only get a fraction of these things set up, you will be better off than where you are at right now. It's the path to higher profits.

Whether you want to sell your business one day or you want to have a more profitable asset that attracts more buyers at a higher price. Maybe you want to hand down this business to your kids one day or you just want this business to give you the lifestyle you've always wanted with low stress and high profits, that all can happen with email automation.

You just have to take the first step. If you'd like us to help you, we are standing by and ready. We have a whole team of experts who absolutely live for this stuff. We eat, sleep, and breathe email marketing. It's what we do best. It's our superpower, and we might be able to help you. We'll let you know if we can help you.

We'll show you exactly how you can uncover more revenue and help you just absolutely crush it. Whatever you decide to do, my hope is that you read and use this book, and that it will help you build an awesome business that you love.

Here's How You Can Scale Your Ecommerce Brand While You Sleep

One of the hardest parts of growing an Ecommerce business is scaling to the point where you have enough cash flow and profit margin. A lot of brands watch their profits evaporate as they're forced to pay sky-high acquisition costs while struggling to increase sales. Some business owners think the only answer to their problem is to pump even MORE money into ads when really they should be focusing on their email marketing.

After working behind the scenes with dozens of Ecommerce brands, I've seen that most brands are leaving a lot of money on the table when it comes to email marketing. I wrote this book to help YOU make more money from your email marketing. The system I lay out for you in this book is simple but hyper-profitable. And once it's set up, it's pretty much hands-off. You can sit back, relax, and watch sales roll in.

When you follow my system, you'll turn one-time buyers into loyal fans of your brand who want to buy from you over and over again; all with the power of our email automation.

If you have found the insights I have shared with you to be of value and would like to learn more, here's what you do next:

Step 1: Go to my website, **TheEmailCopywriter.com** and sign up for my list. I share email marketing tips every single day that you're going to love.

Step 2: Subscribe to my print newsletter, Make It Rain Monthly where I share my best strategies for making more sales with email: **MakeItRainMonthly.com**

Step 3: Go to **www.orzymedia.com** and apply to work with my team. We can take over your email marketing and grow your revenue fast.

We'll help you make MORE sales without paying expensive acquisition costs so you can have more cash flow in your business, more money in your pocket, and a lot less stress in your life.

Made in United States
Troutdale, OR
05/23/2024